INTEGRITY
PLAYBOOK

FELLOWSHIP OF CHRISTIAN ATHLETES

INTEGRITY PLAYBOOK

TRUE CHAMPIONS TALK ABOUT THE HEART AND SOUL IN SPORTS

Revell

a division of Baker Publishing Group
Grand Rapids, Michigan

© 2008, 2015 by Fellowship of Christian Athletes

Published by Revell
a division of Baker Publishing Group
P.O. Box 6287, Grand Rapids, MI 49516-6287
www.revellbooks.com

Material adapted from *Integrity*, published in 2008 by Regal Books.

ISBN 978-0-8007-2674-4

Printed in the United States of America

Unless otherwise indicated, Scripture quotations are from the Holman Christian Standard Bible, copyright 1999, 2000, 2002, 2003 by Holman Bible Publishers. Used by permission.

Scripture quotations labeled NIV are from the Holy Bible, New International Version®. NIV®. Copyright © 1973, 1978, 1984, 2011 by Biblica, Inc.™ Used by permission of Zondervan. All rights reserved worldwide. www.zondervan.com

15 16 17 18 19 20 21   7 6 5 4 3 2

Contents

The Four Core

DAN BRITTON

*Executive Vice President of
International Ministry, Fellowship
of Christian Athletes*

The NCAA Final Four tournament is an exciting sporting event. Even if you are not a person who likes basketball, it is awesome to watch March Madness as it narrows down sixty-four teams into four core teams. This makes me think about Fellowship of Christian Athlete's "Four Core"—not four core teams, but four core values.

Core values are simply the way you live and conduct yourself. They are your attitudes, beliefs and convictions. Values should be what you are, not what you want to become. The goal is to embody your values every step of the way.

Are your values just words, or do you actually live them out? Can others identify the values in your life without you telling them? Your values need to be a driving force that shapes the way you do life! Talk is cheap, but values are valuable.

When everything is stripped away, what is left? For FCA, it is integrity, serving, teamwork, and excellence. These Four Core are so powerful to me that I have made them my own personal values. So, I have to ask you, what are your values? What guides you? Let me share with you FCA's Four Core, which are even better than the Final Four!

Integrity

To have integrity means that you are committed to Christlike wholeness, both privately and publicly. Basically, it means to live without gaps. Proverbs 11:3 says that integrity should guide you, but that a double life will destroy you. You need to be transparent, authentic, honest, and trustworthy. You should be the same in all situations and not become someone different when the competition of the game begins. Integrity means to act the same when no one is looking as you do when all eyes are on you. It is not about being perfect, but, as a coach or athlete, you need to be the real deal.

Serving

In John 13:12–15, Jesus gives us the perfect example of serving when He washes the disciples' feet. He then commands the disciples to go and do unto others what

He has done to them. How many of your teammates' feet have you washed? Maybe not literally, but spiritually, do you have an attitude of serving just as if you were washing their feet in the locker room? You need to seek out the needs of others and be passionate about pursuing people who are needy. And, the last time I checked, everyone is needy.

Teamwork

Teamwork means to work together with others and express unity in Christ in all of your relationships. In Philippians 2:1–5, Paul encourages each of us to be one, united together in spirit and purpose. We all need to be on one team—not just the team we play on, but on God's Team! We need to equip, encourage, and empower one another. Do you celebrate and hurt together as teammates? You need to be arm-in-arm with others, locking up together to accomplish God's work. There should be no Lone Rangers.

Excellence

To pursue excellence means to honor and glorify God in everything you do. In Colossians 3:23–24, Paul writes, "whatever you do, work at it with all your heart, as working for the Lord, not for men." The "whatever" part is hard, because it means that everything you do must be done for God, not others. You need to pursue excellence in practice, in games, in schoolwork and in lifting weights. God deserves your best, not your leftovers.

It is tip-off time for the game of life. How will you be known?

Introduction

The Gap

Whatever happens, conduct your-
selves in a manner worthy of the
gospel of Christ.

> Philippians 1:27 NIV

I know, my God, that you test the
heart and are pleased with integrity. All these things have I given
willingly and with honest intent.

> 1 Chronicles 29:17

Lord Jesus, my prayer is to live and compete with integrity, serving, teamwork, and excellence. It is a high standard, but I know that with Your power and strength, it can happen. I want all my relationships to be known for things that are of You. Search my heart and reveal to me my values. I lay at the foot of the cross the values that do not honor You, and I ask for Your forgiveness. The values that bring You glory, I lay at the foot of the cross for Your anointing.

The core value of integrity is more than the classic definition of "who we are when no one is watching." Integrity is a value that we need to pursue, even when it is not convenient. It ultimately defines us. Our talk, decisions, thoughts, and actions are built on our integrity.

Integrity takes a lifetime to build and a second to lose. We are always one decision away from being stupid. When we maintain a life of integrity, there is wholeness of soul. There is spiritual and emotional rest.

There are no spiritual shortcuts to integrity. Being committed to live out daily what we believe takes spiritual sweat. As legendary Hall of Fame basketball coach John Wooden once said, "A leader's most powerful ally is his or her own example. There is hypocrisy to the phrase, 'Do as I say, not as I do.' I refused to make demands on my boys that I wasn't willing to live out in my own life."

Integrity is not about being perfect, but about being transparent and authentic. Sometimes nonbelievers have more integrity than Christians. For them, it is "what you see is what you get!" They do not hide anything. The world is dying to see authentic followers of Christ. God desires for us to have spiritual authenticity, not spiritual duplicity.

Too often, we desire to live a life that we know we have not committed in our hearts to living. We also want others to do as we say, not as we do. What I mean by this is that we desire our external life (the life that everyone sees—our wins and accomplishments) to be greater than our internal life (the life that no one sees—our thoughts and desires).

The two key ingredients of integrity are honesty and truth. When these become merely an option and not a non-negotiable standard, gaps develop in our integrity, and hypocrisy is born. The best definition of "hypocrisy" I have ever heard is that it is "the gap that exists between the public life and the private life." It is the difference between the external life and the internal life.

There is a constant war in our souls. We do not want others to see us as we really are. We are afraid that the gap will be exposed. However, God desires the exact opposite. He wants us to bring the dark things—the things that we have buried in our hearts—into the light so that He can purify us. He wants every aspect of our lives to be filled with integrity.

Oswald Chambers once wrote, "My worth to God in public is only what I am in private." Be committed to being real—gap-free!

How to Use this Book

Integrity Playbook takes an in-depth look at this core value and comes at it from six different angles as lived out by six different people. Their insights shed new light on this value and give us a model to follow.

You can read *Integrity Playbook* individually or as part of a group. As part of a personal devotion time, you can gain insight as you read through each story and ponder the "Training Time" questions at the end. Mentors can also use this book in a discipleship relationship, using the "Training Time" questions to step up conversations to the next level. And small groups (huddles) can study the core value as a group to be prepared to sharpen each other with questions.

1

The Quest for Consistency

TONY DUNGY

*Winning Super Bowl Coach
of the Indianapolis Colts*

Remember your leaders who have spoken God's word to you. As you carefully observe the outcome of their lives, imitate their faith. Jesus Christ is the same yesterday, today, and forever.

Hebrews 13:7–8

It is not what we eat but what we digest that makes us strong; not what we gain but what we save that makes us rich; not what we read but what we remember that makes us learned; and not what we profess but what we practice that gives us integrity.

Francis Bacon

Living in full view of the microscopic public eye can test the will of even the strongest of characters. Tony Dungy

can certainly attest to that brutal truth.
As the celebrated former head coach of
the Indianapolis Colts, he's experienced
the pinnacle of success, the most tragic
of personal losses, and everything in
between.

For the average Joe, experiencing a few
highs and lows with nondescript days in
between is simply called "life." But for
Dungy—when every detail is reported,
discussed, prognosticated, and opined—
life is something completely different and
looks more like a virtual three-ring circus
in which triumphs and defeats are fodder
for the masses.

That's why integrity is so vital in the
life of the Christian. After all, everyone
is in the public eye to some degree, with
followers of Christ attracting much of the
scrutinizing spotlight. And that's what
makes Dungy so special. Now back in
the spotlight as an NFL analyst for NBC
Sports, his integrity is unwavering, his
character rock solid—no matter what

circumstance comes his way. It's a quality that people can't help but notice from up close and from far away.

"The greatest things I have learned from Coach Dungy would have to be humility and consistency," former Indianapolis tight end Ben Utecht says. "He truly leads by example, and he does it consistently. This allows people to really see his faith every single day, and that's the most important thing."

Not only do his players recognize Dungy's steady approach, but the men and women who cover the national sports scene also are amazed at his impeccable commitment to doing the right thing.

"Tony Dungy is probably the most even-keeled person I have ever met," ESPN anchor Chris Berman says. "In the span of just over a year, he experienced a personal low that can get no lower—the tragic death of his son—and the professional high that can be no higher—winning the Super Bowl. The way he carried himself in both situations, you wouldn't know the difference, really, in what event just occurred. I don't know many people who could do that. I love him for his fortitude and his unbelievable ability to stay the course."

"Tony is a man of such inner strength that you can't help but be inspired by him," NBC *Sunday Night Football* reporter Michelle Tafoya adds. "He is consistent, composed and compassionate. I've never met another coach like him, and I don't expect to. From Tony, I have learned that you can be successful while maintaining your integrity, that you can be composed while being competitive, and that you can leave a legacy based on character."

Those strong words are echoed by countless others and reflect the sentiment of people who have observed Dungy's nearly thirty years within the coaching ranks. Amazingly, all but one year of his entire career took place inside the demanding confines of the National Football League, where coaches are required to spend eighty hours a week on the job just to have a sniff at success and where character and integrity are challenged on a daily basis.

Yet somehow, Dungy served as a head coach from 1996 to 2008 and managed not only to maintain a high standard of integrity but also to become a role model of character for coaches and athletes at every level of competition—from the Pee Wee League all the way to the NFL.

"Integrity, to me, is what you are all about," Dungy says. "It's what's inside of you. And what's inside is eventually going to come out when it gets to a critical situation. That, to me, is the difference between a championship team and just a good team. That's the difference between a person you really want to follow and someone who is just another person in your life. With people of integrity, you know what you are going to get because that person is the same way all the time; situations don't change them. That's what I look for in players, and that's what I want to give players from a leadership standpoint—that they can count on me to be the same no matter what. Being the same is not just being mediocre. It's really being the person that God wants you to be all the time."

Dungy's legacy of integrity began not as a coach but as a player. The Michigan native was the starting quarterback at the University of Minnesota from 1973 to 1976 and spent his freshman season playing on the basketball team as well. As a free agent, he signed with the Pittsburgh Steelers as a defensive back. He was later converted to wide receiver and then to safety. In his second season, Dungy took part in the Steelers' 35–31 victory over Dallas in Super Bowl XIII.

After two years in Pittsburgh and one year in San Francisco, Dungy returned to his alma mater to coach the defensive backs for a season. By 1981, he was back in the NFL for good. After assistant coaching stints in Pittsburgh, Kansas City, and Minnesota, his sphere of influence expanded when he was named head coach of the Tampa Bay Buccaneers. And while the demands on his life increased, so too did notice of his ability to display grace under fire. The assistant coaches and support staff that surrounded him were particularly quick to see this.

One of those impressionable co-workers was Les Steckel, who served as Tony Dungy's offensive coordinator in Tampa Bay for the 2000 season. Steckel, who is now president of the Fellowship of Christian Athletes, learned quickly how his former boss's word consistently reflected his integrity—so much so that he never questioned anything Dungy said.

"Someone had told me that Tony had memorized the book of James," Steckel recalls. "I went up to Tony after practice one day during the summer and I said,

THE QUEST FOR CONSISTENCY **27**

'Hey, Tony, I hear you memorized the book of James this summer.' And he said, 'Yeah.' That's all he said, and I didn't ask him anything else. He said, 'Yeah,' and I believed him."

After turning the Buccaneers organization into a winner (even falling just six points shy of a berth in Super Bowl XXXIV), he was sought out by Indianapolis Colts' owner Jim Irsay to replace Jim Mora. Irsay says that Dungy reminded him of the legendary Dallas Cowboys' coach Tom Landry. He was impressed by Dungy's ability to win with integrity and saw him as the visionary who could lead the Colts to the NFL's Promised Land.

"The most important quality for any head coach is to be the leader of men," Irsay says. "Tony has those qualities. He never shies away from difficult circumstances. He's very pragmatic in terms of the way he looks at things.

"He has a lot of street smarts, and he's extremely competitive. The fires burn in there deeply, and people demonstrate that in different ways. But he's as competitive as Lombardi or any coach who might have been more outward with their emotions. He's very intelligent. He has a great understanding of the game. He grew up under great teachers, so all of those things were there to give him the pedigree to make him a Hall of Fame NFL coach."

While Dungy would surely blush at Irsay's words of praise, he would also be hard pressed to reject his team-owner's assertion that integrity and consistency play a vital role in the success of any coach. Dungy says that holds especially true with more experienced athletes who require larger doses of trust in their leaders.

"Sometimes I think when you're dealing with younger players—junior high, high school—they're going to follow the coach because he's the authority figure," Dungy says. "They've been taught that they just have to follow that adult figure. But when you're dealing with professional athletes and college athletes, that goes out the window. They're going to follow you because they believe in you, and they see something that causes them to follow you. So I think it's even more important for us to build those relationships for our players and to not be anything different than they think we are because they're not going to buy into it, and they're not going to follow you wholeheartedly if there are any chinks in the armor."

For Dungy, his intense desire to live a life of integrity began at an early age. His parents, Dr. Wilbur and CleoMae Dungy, were both educators in Jackson, Michigan, where Dungy was born and raised. Although both have since passed on, their example of honesty, character, and integrity continues to inspire him to always do what's right in the eyes of God.

While coaching in Tampa, Dungy took his commitment to integrity within the family a step further by helping cofound a program called All Pro Dads—a division of a larger organization known as Family First. The group hosts special events at various NFL stadiums and encourages fathers to step up their commitment in the home. Taking part in such an organization is a natural extension of the kind of parent Dungy strives to be in his own family.

"It's very important to let my family know that here are our standards," Dungy says. "Here are the Lord's standards. This is what we're going to try to live up to. Sure we're going to fail at times. We're going to fall short. But this is our role model. This is what we're all about. This is what people can expect to see hopefully all the time. And I think that's very important. Your family sees a lot more of you than your players do. If you're not totally transparent, and if you're not totally honest and have that integrity at home, then it's going to show up sooner there than it does at work."

During the 2005 season, Dungy's integrity as a father was put to an unexpected and life-altering test. His oldest son, James, who was attending college in Tampa at the time, took his own life. The quest for a Super Bowl title suddenly came to a screeching halt as Dungy was forced to temporarily step away from his duties as head coach and focus all of his energy on being the spiritual leader of his heartbroken home.

At James's funeral, Dungy showed incredible poise and grace. Hundreds of family members, friends, and associates (past and present) marveled at the peace that enveloped this grieving father. After the service, Les Steckel recalls a brief encounter with Dungy. The two embraced, and Dungy whispered into his friend's ear, "Nobody told me being a Christian would be this hard."

In his book *Quiet Strength: The Principles, Practices, and Priorities of a*

Winning Life, Dungy admits later feeling as if his credibility as spokesman for All Pro Dads and supporter of other family-related organizations and ministries might be diminished because of what might be perceived as a parental failure. But his thoughts turned to the Bible story of Job—a man who was above reproach yet suffered through some of the most tragic sets of circumstances ever recorded.

As described in the biblical book, Satan asked God to remove His hand of protection from Job. It was Satan's belief that if Job were to suffer great misfortune, he would ultimately curse God. Satan proceeded to destroy everything of value in Job's life. Job certainly questioned God during this time of tribulation, but much to Satan's surprise and dismay, Job never turned his back on the Lord.

Ultimately, God blessed Job for his faithfulness, not just by restoring his life, but also by giving him back twice as much as he had lost.

Dungy's personal loss may not have been as severe, but no doubt God has blessed him for staying faithful to the pursuit of integrity in the aftermath of such a devastating loss. The following season, in fact, Dungy experienced the pinnacle of success by leading the Colts to victory at Super Bowl XLI. In the process, he became the first African-American NFL coach to win the prestigious game.

And if Dungy wasn't already a beloved national figure, that single crowning achievement suddenly opened the floodgates for a whole new world of opportunity and influence. "That's the great thing about winning," Irsay says. "It gives you a stage. It gives you a podium where you can have a chance to demonstrate the virtues that are important to you."

Dungy agrees, but he warns that such a platform can also be treacherous to occupy if its foundation isn't cemented by one's commitment to integrity. And it's not about protecting an individual's image or salvaging self-respect and pride. Dungy says that his desire to live out integrity before others is rooted in a significant calling on his life, a calling that is shared by all who claim Jesus as their Savior.

"It is very important for a Christian athlete or a Christian coach to model integrity," Dungy says. "Because once I have gone out there and said, 'I am a Christian—here are the principles I live by,' if I do anything that undermines that, that's hurting the cause of Christ, that's hurting the gospel. It would be better off for me not to say anything. But once people know I am a Christian, I can't afford to walk differently than I believe because everybody is going to see, especially in a high-profile position like a college coach, a high-school coach, a professional coach. Eyes are on you all the time."

It's a scenario that brings to mind another image of Job—when his so-called friends criticized him and searched for the sins and failures that must have led to such devastating circumstances. But Dungy knows well that judgment and opposition can come even during the good times. In November 2004, *Monday Night Football* aired a racy pregame skit in which Terrell Owens (then with the Philadelphia Eagles) costarred with *Desperate Housewives* actress Nicollette Sheridan. Dungy made a point to publicly denounce the skit for its immoral content, but his complaint was taken out of context when he mentioned his disappointment in Owens for furthering negative stereotypes about black athletes and sexual conduct.

In those moments, Dungy has been able to take his lead from the example of Jesus Christ, who during His ministry on Earth was constantly challenged by the religious leaders of the day—in particular the Pharisees—for teachings that shook the foundations of popular belief.

But unlike Jesus, who was a sinless and perfect man, Dungy quickly owns up to the reality of his own imperfections. In those times when he does make a mistake, he is all too aware of the ramifications—especially for the follower of Christ.

"It's really tough," Dungy admits. "It's tough on me when I don't follow through with what I say I'm going to do or if I do something different or something that I know is wrong. It's really hurtful, because I know that eventually that's going to come to light and not only make my job tougher, but more than that, it's going to cause people to question what Christianity is about."

And because of this honest recognition of his own humanity, Dungy finds it much easier to forgive and forget the trespasses of others around him. "I have a tendency to forgive people because that's what Christ is all about," Dungy says. "I've worked in situations where once you lose that integrity from your boss, you don't really look at them the same way; and you're still going to go out there and give it everything you've got, but something's a little bit different, and I don't want that to happen for me and the people I work with."

As the former punter for Indianapolis, Hunter Smith saw firsthand the disciplined but gentle manner in which Dungy handled problems that arose within the team setting. It's an approach that he says stood out in the rough-and-tumble world of the NFL.

"In a profession that is full of reactions, Coach Dungy has chosen to be a responder, and he responds as Christ would respond," Smith says. "Jesus didn't react to the people who came against Him; He responded to them in love, humility, and justice. That's how I feel Coach Dungy runs his family, his team, and his life."

Not surprisingly, Dungy's strong convictions regarding forgiveness and compassion—even for those who have failed to maintain a high level of integrity—are based first and foremost on the example set by Christ. It is Christ's unwavering consistency, described in all four Gospels, that challenges Dungy to live in a similar manner before his family, his team, and the general public.

And despite the culture's growing amorality and indifference, Dungy holds firm to his belief that character still matters and that following Jesus's consistent model of integrity is the only way to maintain a clean reputation before men and, more importantly, before God.

"We have so many pressures coming at us that tempt us not to live up to our integrity," Dungy says. "It's so easy to say nowadays, 'Well, everybody else is doing it,' or to think it's not important to be 100 percent accurate and honest and truthful because, after all, winning is the most important thing. We're under that pressure, but you know what? My integrity is first, and it doesn't matter if we win or not. I'm not going to let anything jeopardize my integrity."

Training Time

1. Tony Dungy says that integrity is "what's inside of you." Describe a critical situation in which your character was brought to the forefront. Were you pleased or displeased with how you reacted?

2. Dungy has experienced the highest highs and the lowest lows, but people have always noted his consistent integrity. Do you find it easier to maintain integrity when things are going well or when things are going poorly?

3. Dungy says, "It's tough on me when I don't follow through with what I say I'm going to do or if I do something . . . that I know is wrong." How do you feel when you break commitments or make mistakes? What kind of effects do those actions have on your integrity?

4. Read Hebrews 13:7–8. What advice is given in this passage? Who are

some spiritual leaders that you look up to as an example of integrity? What can you learn about integrity through the life of Jesus?

5. Francis Bacon once said that it's "not what we profess but what we practice that gives us integrity." What are some examples of talking the talk but not walking the walk? How important is it to practice integrity and not just profess it? How might the practice of integrity help with consistency?

journal

journal

2

Unashamed

Rocco Grimaldi
NHL Center

My eager expectation and hope is that I will not be ashamed about anything, but that now as always, with all boldness, Christ will be highly honored in my body, whether by life or by death.

Philippians 1:20

Cowardice asks the question, "Is it safe?" Expediency asks the question, "Is it politic?" Vanity asks the question, "Is it popular?" But, conscience asks the question, "Is it right?" And there comes a time when one must take a position that is neither safe, nor politic, nor popular but one must take it because one's conscience tells one that it is right.

Martin Luther King Jr.

It may be a stretch to say with certainty that Rocco Grimaldi was born to play hockey. But sometimes the facts are just too hard to ignore. Take, for instance, the fact that Grimaldi first strapped on a pair of roller skates to play roller hockey when he was four years old and, in less than a year, he had found his way to the ice.

"I got involved in sports at a young age and was playing baseball when I first discovered hockey," Grimaldi recalls. "Hockey just seemed so much faster. There was a lot more going, and as an active kid, I fell in love with the sport right away."

That wasn't the only love that Grimaldi discovered at the age of four. Perhaps not coincidentally, he also accepted Jesus as his Savior that same year.

"All of my passions kicked in right away," he quips.

Over the next several years, Grimaldi's commitment to both hockey and the Christian faith continued to grow. His athletic ability was especially evident very early in the process. Grimaldi joined his first travel team when he was five and advanced to the point where he was competing with players twice his age. After a successful stint with the California Wave, his family moved to Michigan so he could consistently play against better competition in the hockey-crazed northern United States. Grimaldi calls it "the second best decision of my life after accepting Christ."

His junior career produced three state championships and two national championships. Grimaldi eventually earned a spot on the US National Team where he won a U17 World Championship gold medal and two U18 World Championship gold medals. From there, he accepted a scholarship offer to play for a perennial NCAA Division I powerhouse at the University of North Dakota.

In 2011, Florida selected Grimaldi with the thirty-third pick in the second round of the NHL Draft. Three years later, he left school a year early and signed a professional contract to play for the Panthers, where he saw his first NHL action during the 2014-15 season. It was a humbling reminder of why he plays the game in the first place.

"God has given me the talent to play hockey," Grimaldi explains. "He didn't give me that talent to be used so I could become famous. Hockey is a platform. It's something that I have to use as a podium from which I can portray why I'm here. I want to tell people about Jesus and how He's the coolest person they'll ever meet. Hockey is just a platform for me to preach the gospel. It's not about me. It's all about Him."

Grimaldi takes the opportunity to influence athletes, coaches, and fans very seriously. Even early in his collegiate career, he became known for his bold approach to sharing his faith with others. Grimaldi sees hockey as a gift and not something that should define his life.

"I could live without hockey," he says. "But while I'm playing, I can use it to share the message of salvation and God's love with a lot of people that would never hear it otherwise."

For Grimaldi, it all boils down to boldness and, as he describes it, being "totally unashamed of Christ."

"A bold Christian isn't going to hide that they believe in Him," he continues. "A bold Christian is going to let people know that Jesus is their life and the reason for living. Whether it's something I say or how I act, I have to reflect Christ. I'm not going to be afraid to say something or be afraid of people criticizing me or putting me down for my faith. Persecution is going to come. He already warned us about that in the Bible."

Grimaldi is referring to the time when Jesus taught His disciples that, "If they persecuted Me, they will also persecute you" (John 15:20).

Like the disciples, Grimaldi has come to understand the importance of being bold despite the unpleasant criticism and name-calling that often follows. But it doesn't have to be a difficult decision if we have a greater understanding of the big picture.

"Boldness happens when you know who you are and you know your place in Christ," Grimaldi explains. "This world is hurt and it's dying. We need voices to step up and start proclaiming the gospel of Christ with boldness."

Stories from the New Testament and the heroes of the early church give Grimaldi the courage to be unashamed to live out his faith. It should be no surprise that one of his favorite scriptures comes from the Apostle Paul, which talks specifically about living boldly for Christ.

"For I am not ashamed of the gospel, because it is God's power for salvation to everyone who believes, first to the Jew, and also to the Greek." (Romans 1:16)

"It didn't matter if [the apostles] were put in jail," Grimaldi says. "It didn't matter if they were beaten. It didn't matter if they were shipwrecked. They trusted in Him and didn't let the world tear them down."

Grimaldi has especially been inspired through the example that John the Baptist set while paving the way for Jesus's ministry.

"John the Baptist was not someone that the world considered special," Grimaldi notes. "He dressed strangely and ate strange food. He didn't have any special gifting. But he was boldly preaching the truth. He didn't care what people said or what they thought. He said what God told him to say no matter how uncool it was, no matter how undesirable it was, or no matter how bad people hated him."

Jesus also was persecuted when He was falsely accused, falsely convicted, brutally tortured, and hung on a cross where He died for the sins of the world. That remains the ultimate display of boldness.

"What Jesus did took so much courage," Grimaldi says. "He laid all of his pride down. He was unashamed His whole life while preaching the gospel. He had boldness in knowing it was God's plan for Him to die. There was no other way. He was so bold in his love for us. He knew what His job was and He stayed strong in doing it."

It's one thing to understand who you are in Christ and to take that knowledge as empowerment to live boldly and unashamedly for the sake of the gospel. But none of that will matter without the presence of godly character and integrity. Paul wrote about this spiritual principle in his letter to the Christians in Philippi.

> "My eager expectation and hope is that I will not be ashamed about anything, but that now as always, with all boldness, Christ will be highly honored in my body, whether by life or by death." (Philippians 1:20)

In other words, when we live with integrity, it empowers us to live boldly and deflates the criticisms from those who might seek to accuse us of hypocrisy. Criticism will come. Boldness often strikes a nerve with people who aren't ready and willing to embrace the good news of the gospel.

Grimaldi discovered that harsh reality in 2011 when he shared a pair of controversial messages via Twitter. First, he addressed his female followers about the issue of modesty. Then, he followed with a strong warning to men about the dangers of lust. While some within the sports media and blogosphere quickly shot back with allegations of self-righteousness and pious posturing, Grimaldi was comforted to know that hundreds more were appreciative of his bold stance. Still, he wasn't surprised at the negative reaction.

"The world is going to hate me for what I believe," Grimaldi says. "They hated Christ. But I'm not of this world anymore. So criticism just comes with the territory. There's no way everyone is going to like you and like the things that you are saying."

Since boldness and integrity are intertwined, it stands to reason that the best foundation for living out both principles is to have a clear understanding of the Bible. It is within those divinely inspired pages where the wisdom and encouragement to live unashamedly and do things the right way can be found.

"You have to know what His Word says before you can live it out," Grimaldi succinctly states.

He's not alone in that opinion. In fact, David shared a similar sentiment.

"I have treasured Your word in my heart so that I may not sin against You." (Psalm 119:11)

And then, Jesus demonstrated this truth when He fasted for 40 days in the wilderness. At the end of His time of preparation, Satan tried to take advantage of Jesus's weakened body and tempted Him on three separate occasions. But each time, He countered with three powerful words: "It is written" (Matthew 4:4-10).

After quoting God's Word as a defense against Satan's scheme, Jesus was able to maintain His integrity and remain sinless. Through the power of God's Word, Jesus launched His ministry and boldly and unashamedly preached the gospel message that is still alive and relevant today.

Just as Jesus courageously completed His mission—even all the way to the cross—we too are called to be unwavering in our convictions, maintain our integrity, and fearlessly live out our faith in a way that makes a difference in the world around us. Grimaldi believes that this kind of life will produce eternal fruit that we may not see until we're in Heaven.

"When we get there someday, I believe that we'll see many people that we touched and led to Christ through our example of integrity and because we were bold enough to share the gospel with them," Grimaldi says. "We have to stay strong. If our teammates or our opponents hate us for it, that doesn't matter. We can have peace in knowing that He is with us. Jesus is the only reason we live."

Training Time

1. What is your definition of "boldness?" On a scale of 1 to 10, how would you rate your boldness in the following areas: A) when sharing personal opinions, B) when engaged in social activities, and C) when sharing your faith?

2. Grimaldi believes that "you have to know what (the Bible) says before you can live it out." How can a strong knowledge of God's Word increase your boldness when sharing your faith with others?

3. In what ways are boldness and integrity linked? Do you think it's

possible to be bold in your faith without integrity?

4. What are some ways that a lack of integrity might harm your ability to be bold in your faith?

5. What are some ways that you can strengthen the integrity in your life today and speak with more boldness about what Jesus has done in your life?

3

Faithful and True

TAMIKA CATCHINGS
WNBA All-Star and Three-Time Olympic Gold Medalist

Never let loyalty and faithfulness leave you. Tie them around your neck; write them on the tablet of your heart.

Proverbs 3:3

Loyalty is the foundational quality that gets us through hard times. Will we compromise our integrity when temptation is great? Or will we remain loyal to our beliefs and core values?

John Wooden

Perhaps it's a cynical perspective, but modern society as a whole seems to be becoming less interested in such noble concepts as loyalty and faithfulness. With each passing day, commitment is increasingly lacking in business, athletics, government, church, and personal relationships.

That's one of the reasons why perennial WNBA All-Star Tamika Catchings tends to stand out in a crowd. Throughout her basketball career, she has earned a reputation as consistently steadfast in her devotion to the game and the people she loves.

But it was an injury at the University of Tennessee that first helped her make the connection between the true meaning of loyalty and devotion to God.

"It might sound crazy, but tearing my ACL in January 2001 was a good thing," Catchings says. "At the time, I wouldn't have agreed. The timing was horrible. My dream was to play in the WNBA, and with just five months until the draft, I was afraid that the injury was going to cost me my dream."

Before the injury, Catchings admits that basketball had become her god. It was all she thought about. It consumed her dreams. Catchings was a good student in school, but at the end of day, it was all about basketball. There was nothing more important in her life.

"When I got hurt, it was like God was telling me to slow down and check my priorities," Catchings says. "He knew that basketball was my life and He used basketball to get me to that point. But that wasn't all He wanted for me. He wanted our relationship to grow as well."

During her time away from basketball, Catchings had plenty of opportunities to reflect on where she was at spiritually. It also allowed her to reprioritize her life. Basketball was still important, but a recommitment to her faith in Christ put things back in their proper order and paved the way for a more fulfilling life. And as she learned more about what it meant to be faithful to God, He in turn was faithful to her. Despite the doctor's report that Catchings would sit out an entire season, the Indiana Fever took a chance on her with the third overall pick of the 2001 WNBA Draft.

"Even while I was still recovering, I was calm and had peace, because I knew that God had a purpose for me to fulfill by playing in the WNBA," she says. "He was with me every step of the way. That entire season, I went to practice every day and just watched. There were days when I woke up and didn't feel like doing it anymore. I'd cry myself to sleep. But deep in my heart, I knew I could make it."

Catchings' ACL injury wasn't the first time she had faced adversity. As a young girl, Catchings struggled with hearing loss and had to wear a hearing aid. She also had a speech problem as well as more typical adolescent frustrations such as wearing glasses and getting braces.

Basketball became her escape. Because there were few opportunities for women's basketball players to compete beyond college, Catchings often dreamt of playing in the NBA like her father Harvey, who spent eleven seasons with four teams and another two years playing professionally in Italy. That led her to Tennessee, where she received even more preparation for life from legendary head coach Pat Summitt.

"Coach Summitt wanted us to be more than just basketball players," Catchings recalls. "Most coaches recruit players to play basketball and do well in school. But to her, it was also about being active in the community and preparing us to be better once we left school."

Catchings was pretty good on the court, too. She won an NCAA championship during her freshman season and finished her career as a four-time All-American. The sense of loyalty she experienced with the Volunteers carried over into her starring role with the Indiana Fever, where she has won a WNBA title and been named league MVP, and her efforts as a three-time Olympic gold medalist with the US National Team. Some additional obstacles only served to fuel her faithfulness to the game and to her Creator.

"During my basketball career, I've suffered other injuries like a torn meniscus and a torn Achilles," Catchings explains. "When I faced those tough times, it would have been easier to give up. But no matter what the circumstance, I've had a strong desire to remain loyal to myself, to my family, to my teams, and to our fans. Most importantly, I want to be loyal to my values and loyal to God. I represent Him in everything I do."

When things haven't gone according to plan, Catchings has found inspiration in the Old Testament account of a young Jewish woman named Esther who was chosen to be Persian king Xerxes' queen. When Haman, one of the king's men, plotted to destroy the Jews, Esther's cousin Mordecai warned her and told her she was the only one who could stop this from happening.

"At that point, Esther could have easily turned her back on Mordecai and her own people," Catchings says. "She could have said, 'No, I'm fine. I'm here in the temple. I don't need any help.' But she took a stand and risked her life in order to save them all."

In Esther 4:14, Mordecai suggested to Esther that perhaps she had been raised up by God "for such a time as this." But that wouldn't have mattered if she had allowed fear and selfishness to compromise her beliefs.

Catchings has never faced such a life-and-death scenario, but she does feel compelled to live out her faith in such a way that people will see the reflection of Christ.

"I've played all over the world in many different countries with different teams," Catchings says. "When I leave those places, I don't know if I'll ever come back. But I want the people there to remember that I had a certain kind of strength about me and that I lived by my Christian principles. Whether I'm playing in Korea, Russia, Turkey, or right here in the United States, I want to be an example of someone who never caves to the pressure of compromise."

The opposite of compromise is loyalty and faithfulness. Catchings has always tried her best to live out those principles in the public eye, especially when using her platform to impact young people across Indianapolis through the Catch The Stars Foundation, an organization whose mission is to help kids "catch their dreams one star at a time," through mentoring, fitness, and educational programs.

"One of the things we always come back to is being able to work with other people," Catchings says. "We put kids together that have never been together in their life. While they're at the camp, they learn to work with that team and that person. With our mentoring program, the focus is helping young people to leave after the six weeks with a greater level of confidence and self-esteem. We've had young girls come to the program and literally not say a word that first week. They keep their heads down and never look anyone in the eye. You wonder if they even want to be there. But by the end of the program, these kids are like flowers that have blossomed. It's amazing to see that."

In order to achieve greatness as a basketball player and as a community leader, Catchings has embraced King Solomon's advice found in Proverbs 3:3: "Never let loyalty and faithfulness leave you. Tie them around your neck; write them on the tablet of your heart."

Catchings has learned that living with integrity becomes much easier when loyalty and faithfulness are inseparable from all areas of her life. This compels her to be the same person in public that she is in private.

"People often ask me what I had to change to get to this level," Catchings says. "They ask what it's like to be a role model. But for me, what you see is what you get. I'm don't have to do anything special or change to become a role model. I live my life like this all the time. This is who I am. This is the whole package. That's how all leaders should be."

And in order to maintain that consistent walk with God and that loyal approach to all of her relationships, Catchings has a few simple things that keep her grounded and committed.

"I stay in the Word," she says. "And the people around me are not 'yes' people. If I mess up or do something wrong, I expect them to correct me and set me straight. My friends and family members also provide a great support group that reminds me what my goals are and what I want to achieve. They help me stay focused."

Catchings knows that fame is fleeting and that one mistake can quickly destroy one's character. That's why integrity, as exemplified through loyalty and faithfulness, is such an important part of her daily walk and vital to helping her fulfill the greater purpose to which she has been called.

"I've been blessed with this platform," Catchings says. "I want to use it to share the adversity I've been through with people who need to hear the message of hope. Because of the expectations I have for my life, I want to be loyal to myself, to my family, to my team, and to our fans. But most importantly, I want to be loyal to God. I represent Him in everything I do."

Training Time

1. What are some specific ways in which you would agree that "modern society as a whole seems to be becoming less interested in such noble concepts as loyalty and faithfulness?"

2. What is it about loyalty that helps us get through tough times, as Coach John Wooden once suggested? Can

you describe a time when that was true for you?

3. What are some things that have tempted you to compromise your values and beliefs? How did you respond to that temptation?

4. In what ways has God been faithful to you?

5. Tamika Catchings listed some things that help her practice loyalty and faithfulness in her life. What are some practical ideas that might help you do the same and stay true to biblical truths and fulfill God's purpose for your life?

journal

4

Follow the Leader

LES STECKEL
Fellowship of Christian Athletes
President and CEO

For the LORD gives wisdom; from His mouth come knowledge and understanding. He stores up success for the upright; He is a shield for those who live with integrity so that He may guard the paths of justice and protect the way of His loyal followers. Then you will understand righteousness, justice, and integrity—every good path. For wisdom will enter your mind, and knowledge will delight your heart.

Proverbs 2:6–10

As the centuries pass, the evidence is accumulating that, measured by His effect on history, Jesus is the most influential life ever lived on this planet.

Kenneth Scott Latourette

For centuries, mankind has debated this universal question: Are leaders born or are they made? In other words, do people come out of the womb with leadership skills built into their DNA? Or is it the process of life combined with the right environment and proper education and training that help people develop into leaders?

Depending on who is asked, the answer will likely be different, which most likely means that leaders arise in both ways. While some people are born with certain gifts and abilities that might give them an advantage when it comes to leadership, others are not so blessed at birth but instead work hard to overcome whatever obstacles and challenges stand in their way.

But no matter what the answer is, one thing is for certain: Integrity is something that *never* comes naturally. Living a life of integrity goes against human nature. Just watch any toddler, and it's plain to see that doing the right thing must be first taught and then learned and, most importantly, practiced and lived out. And even then, we must still guard ourselves against things that might challenge our integrity.

Les Steckel says that one of the biggest hurdles people face in their quest to have integrity is the temptation to cave in to social pressures due to a natural desire to be accepted. As a former NFL football coach with over 30 years of experience at the collegiate and professional level, he often felt like a lonely outsider as he strived to live out the admonition found in 1 Peter 2:9, which in the King James Version refers to followers of Christ as "a peculiar people."

"There's not a lot of free time in coaching, but when there is, some coaches will go out and do some things that might challenge your integrity," Steckel says. "If you don't go along with those social settings, you may get ostracized, but you feel like you don't have a relationship with them like the others do. . . . It's a life that's different. The Scripture says that we are to be peculiar. You certainly don't want to be perceived that way at times."

According to Steckel—who retired from coaching in 2005 to accept the position of president and CEO of the Fellowship of Christian Athletes—one of the biggest problems our nation is facing is an attack on the foundations of integrity. Basic moral values are being diminished, and many people believe that integrity is nothing more than a synonym for honesty. But Steckel believes it's so much more than that.

"I've always said integrity is weaving your private world together with your public world," he says. "I think a man's reputation is what other men think about him. A man's character is what God knows about him. So the reputation is from his public life, but character is from his private life. Only God knows our lives, and, if we're all honest, we all have secret lives. It's being alert to that; and as you grow older, you become aware of that and you try to deal with it."

For Steckel, it's been a long journey that started in Whitehall, Pennsylvania. One of the most memorable lessons he ever learned took place while he was attending college at the University of Kansas. His family was hardly affluent, so to travel to and from school in Lawrence, Kansas, he would hitchhike.

"One day my mom came to me and said, 'When you get back to KU, you call us collect and you ask for yourself, and that way we'll know you arrived safely,'" Steckel recalls. "And my dad overheard it, and I thought he was going to blast both of us. He went ballistic and said, 'Don't you dare do that. Do you know how dishonest that is, cheating a phone company by fooling them like that?' I was petrified. So I knew that when I got back, I was going to have to pay 70 cents to make a three-minute call on the pay phone. That showed me that if you're going to be honest in the little things, you had better be honest in the big things."

Steckel's education intensified in 1968 when, following his graduation from Kansas, he joined the Marine Corps and then a year later served in Vietnam as an infantry officer. In 1972, he joined the Marine Corps Reserves and served part-time while balancing his coaching career before retiring as a colonel in 1999.

"Being a Marine and spending 30 years in the Marine Corps, I found that they have tremendous principles of discipline and work ethic and esprit de corps and teamwork and camaraderie," Steckel says. "And yet within the ranks, there are always people who, surprisingly, let you down. That's what is challenging for a Christian man who is trying to live a life of integrity but from time to time faces battles he can't handle. That's when pride becomes an issue; and when pride becomes an issue, we try to solve the problems and defeat the opponent by ourselves and not realize that, like the Scripture says [in 2 Corinthians 12:10], when we're weak, God is strong."

Early in his coaching career, Steckel spent time as an assistant at Colorado and Navy before making the leap to the NFL with San Francisco in 1978. He spent 1979 to 1983 as an assistant coach with the Minnesota Vikings before taking over as head coach in 1984. It was a short-lived experience, however, as he was fired following the Vikings' 3–13 season.

Up to that point, Steckel had already been involved in various ministries, including FCA for twelve years. But his understanding of what true integrity really should look like in the life of a Christian man didn't come into focus until 1985, when he joined head coach Raymond Berry's staff at New England. In that first season, the Patriots reached their first ever Super Bowl, which they eventually lost to a legendary Chicago Bears team that featured head coach Mike

Ditka and star athletes Walter Payton, Richard Dent, Mike Singletary, and Jim McMahon.

Despite the hugely successful season, however, it was Berry's quiet, unassuming witness that made the strongest and most lasting impact on Steckel's life.

"Raymond was the greatest Christian model I ever saw," Steckel says. "One thing I knew for sure: When Raymond said something, it was the truth. You never questioned it—ever. When you have models like that in your life, then you want to emulate them. When I saw Raymond, he had qualities of Jesus that were lived out every day."

Steckel takes Berry's life as a model of Jesus, and he compares the qualities he observed in Berry to the "fruit of the spirit" that Paul wrote about in Galatians 5:22–23. "I saw love from Raymond for his players, for his wife and for his children," he says. "He had the patience of Job, and it drove me crazy at times. He showed me tremendous peace. I've never seen a guy in such stressful moments show such signs of peace. He was very gentle. I was so used to other head coaches who were fire and brimstone, and Raymond's talks were so gentle and his peace came through loud and clear. He was kind to everyone. Even the custodians and the parking-lot attendants—he knew those people by their first name. And that was a model for me, so whenever I've gone different places, I've tried to do the same.

"He was faithful," Steckel continues. "I can remember the day of Super Bowl XX. I had this great creative idea to do something in our game plan. I ran to his hotel room down the hall, and there he was in his robe reading his Bible the morning of the Super Bowl. I just thought, *Wow*. That made a real impact on me. And he showed great goodness to everyone."

In short, Berry modeled Christ to Steckel in a way that he had never quite seen before. And that up-close-and-personal viewpoint caused him to rethink the way he was modeling Christ to others around himself. But it wasn't until 1990 that Steckel fully understood what integrity was really all about. At that point, he found himself unemployed after a one-year stint at Brown University. In his autobiography, *One Yard Short: Turning Your Defeats into Victories*, he describes in detail a 13-month period when God shattered him emotionally and spiritually, and then methodically pieced his life back together again.

"Prior to my brokenness in 1990, I'm not sure how much modeling I was doing," Steckel says. "I was doing a lot of talking. Without a doubt, after my brokenness, not only did I want to be an FCA guy, I wanted to model Christ and let people know that's who I was following. And I found it to be a very lonely life. There were times that I would walk into the locker room and there would be an instant hush. It wasn't so much that they were talking about me. They were saying things that they knew they shouldn't be saying, and I happened to be around. It was tough at times, but I tried to live out my priorities. I think a man of integrity needs to know what his priorities are."

"I've always said that my faith came first, and that wasn't true prior to my brokenness," Steckel adds. "My god was football. It wasn't Jesus Christ. But after my brokenness, it certainly changed quickly."

To remind himself of his renewed commitment to Christ-centered priorities, Steckel created a seven-point list that relies on a heavy dose of alliteration: (1) faith, (2) family, (3) football (since replaced by FCA), (4) friends, (5) fitness, (6) finances, and (7) fun.

"When I have to make a decision, I try to be a man of integrity, and I look at my priority list," Steckel says. "I ask myself, *Are you in fact living out your priorities?* and *Are you modeling Christ?*"

One of Steckel's new life verses is found in Proverbs 2:6–10, where Solomon talks about the kind of wisdom that comes only from God and was lived out through Jesus as portrayed in the Gospels. Steckel now had the original template that he needed to walk with divinely inspired integrity that will "guard the paths of justice and protect the way of [God's] loyal followers" (v. 8).

"We have this tremendous integrity modeled that we should try to emulate," Steckel says. "It's hard to emulate when you're not in the Word. So you don't really know who Jesus is except what people tell you. But the more you read about this living Son of God, you understand that integrity is a special character quality that so many people are labeled as having. But do we have Christlike integrity? If you can't emulate the values you believe in, then you're obviously going to have a hard time getting other people to follow you along those lines."

Steckel spent two seasons at Colorado as an assistant coach under Promise Keepers' founder Bill McCartney before returning to the NFL, where he spent time at Denver, Houston, Tennessee, Tampa Bay, and Buffalo. He was able to work alongside such solid Christian head coaches as Jeff Fisher and Tony Dungy. He also enjoyed the opportunity to coach in a second Super Bowl, but his Tennessee Titans lost to the St. Louis Rams in one of the NFL's most exciting championship games.

Still, with a greater commitment to integrity and more accountability support than ever before, Steckel absolutely understood—as he continues to understand today—that he would need to be ready for any attacks that might come against his moral character.

"As a Christian, every day we take the playing field or, to use a military term, we take the battlefield," Steckel says. "If I'm aware of the enemy and what the situation is and who the enemy is, I've got a chance of winning the battles. Every day I wake up, it says in Ephesians I need to put on the armor of Christ—the helmet of salvation, the breastplate of righteousness, the belt of truth, the sandals of a peacemaker, the shield of faith and the sword of the Spirit. If you get out of your bed or out of the rack, as they say in the Marine Corps, without putting on the armor of Christ, you're going to get beat every day."

Once that armor has been donned, Steckel says the believer must then be able to recognize who the enemy is and learn how to fight against the attacks that are certain to come. Those attacks come in three progressively dangerous forms.

"First, there's the secular world," Steckel says. "All you've got to do is listen to people talk, watch television, watch people's actions and the next thing you know the secular world is dictating to you how to act. That's not what God wants us to do. Then there's selfishness. That's the biggest battle that we'll have all our lives, until we crawl into the grave. God talks about that all the time. I share that with my children. If you really want to have a fruitful, exciting Christian experience, you literally have to be totally empty of yourself and fill your life up with the spirit of the living God."

To combat those two enemies of integrity, Steckel recommends a healthy dose of Jesus's admonition in Luke 9:23: "If anyone wants to come with Me, he must deny himself, take up his cross daily, and follow Me."

But when Steckel brings up the third enemy of integrity—Satan—he admits that it sometimes draws some strange responses. "I know there are people out there who hear the term 'Satan' and think, *What are you making this up for?*" Steckel says. "But I can tell you that since I've been called to this position with FCA, I have been more aware of Satan than ever before in my life. There's really a battle. He does not want success to take place. And when he sees it, he just comes at you harder."

So when the temptation to cut corners or take the easy road makes its sly, sneaky entrance—and it assuredly will—Steckel reminds himself and advises others to consider Christ, the ultimate role model of integrity, and how He handled Himself in the face of death itself (see Matt. 26:39).

"There's no greater example of that than Jesus's going to the cross," Steckel says. "He knew that's what He was supposed to do. He had no desire to do it. He cried out to the Lord. But when it gets right down to it, you can have a clear conscience when you know you're living a life of integrity."

Training Time

1. Read Matthew 7:13–14. How would you compare the choice between the wide road and the narrow road to

today's life choices? Why do you think so many take the path of destruction and so few take the road that leads to eternal life?

2. Read 1 Peter 2:9. What does this verse tell you about the kind of life to which Christians have been called? What are some pressures you have personally faced?

3. Steckel calls former New England Patriots head coach Raymond Berry "the greatest Christian model" he has ever known. Read Galatians 5:22–23. What are the "fruits of the spirit" in this passage? How might each one help you in your quest for a life of integrity?

4. When Steckel was offensive coordinator with the Tennessee Titans, he once made the choice to take the responsibility for a poor decision. Can you describe a time when you were faced with a similar decision? How did you ultimately react? How

did that action affect your decisions
from that point forward?
5. Read Proverbs 2:6–10. Who does
this passage suggest is the perfect
example of integrity? What are
some of God's attributes (as exemplified by Christ) by which you
should live?

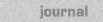

5

Staying the Course

AARON BADDELEY
PGA Golfer

Brothers, I do not consider myself to have taken hold of it. But one thing I do: forgetting what is behind and reaching forward to what is ahead, I pursue as my goal the prize promised by God's heavenly call in Christ Jesus.

Philippians 3:13–14

Never give in, never give in, never, never, never, never—in nothing, great or small, large or petty—never give in except to convictions of honour and good sense.

Winston Churchill

Depending on the golf course, the average PGA golfer will take roughly 280 shots during a four-round tournament. Within each one of those swings there is an enormous amount of pressure. For some players, one shot could make the difference between picking up a weekend paycheck and making an early exit—the difference between retaining a tour card and going back to qualifying school.

Aaron Baddeley fully understands all of the ramifications that accompany golf's micromanaged scoring system. He has missed the cut by one stroke and made the cut by the same paper-thin margin. Baddeley never takes his position on the PGA for granted but somehow finds relief from the inherent stress with a special technique.

"There are times that I get over a shot, and I'm a little worried about it," Baddeley says. "Then you're like, *I don't have a spirit of fear. I've got a spirit of power, love, and a sound mind.* Sometimes I write Scriptures on my glove as a reminder. Sometimes you can get to a certain shot, and you're a little wary about it, and you can quote Scripture, and get a peace about it."

Baddeley's paraphrasing of 2 Timothy 1:7 is a far cry from the lackadaisical attitude toward prayer he maintained throughout most of his life as a teenager and young adult in his early twenties, even though he had parents who set a solid Christian example for him.

Born in Lebanon, New Hampshire, Baddeley's father, Ron, worked as chief mechanic for Mario Andretti's race team. The family moved back to its native Australia when the young Baddeley was nearing his third birthday. To this day, Baddeley enjoys dual citizenship, though he represents Australia in professional golf. Back in Melbourne, he spent the formative years of his childhood in a family that regularly attended a church where his father was an elder and his mom was a Sunday school teacher.

"I remember giving my life to Christ when I was twelve years old," Baddeley says. "I was at a youth outreach where a famous Australian rules football player was speaking. But after that, I just went through the motions."

While a relationship with God quickly became an afterthought, Baddeley's strong desire for athletic competition became king in his life. He started playing golf under the guidance of his grandmother Jean when he was eight years old, but he didn't get serious about the sport until he was fourteen. Up until that point, Baddeley says, he was a serious cricket player.

But once golf finally won him over, Baddeley grew more and more obsessed with it. Not only did he work tirelessly on the fundamentals of the game, but he also began studying the game's history and developing a thirst for knowledge of golf's biggest stars.

"I knew everyone, especially the big names," Baddeley says. "I watched so much golf, it was ridiculous. I could tell you every shot Nick Price hit in the last round when he won the PGA

[Championship] at Southern Hills [in Tulsa, Oklahoma, in 1992]. I could tell you the commentary. Ever since I started playing golf, I just loved watching it."

By the time Baddeley was eighteen, he was one of Australia's top amateur golfers. That fact was solidified when he won the 1999 Australian Open—the youngest player ever to do so. But not long after his crowning achievement, Baddeley fell into a slump. He admits that ten months later, he was tempted to "quit the game." Instead, he decided to recommit himself to golf and defended his title by winning the 2000 Australian Open—this time as a professional.

Five months later, he played in his first PGA Tour event at the Honda Classic. One might assume the college-aged youngster would have been just a little bit intimidated by the prospect of playing alongside golf's greatest players. But that was far from the truth. When he was younger, Baddeley had played with legendary Australian golfer Greg Norman. He also befriended Phil Mickelson; and the two practiced together in Scottsdale, Arizona, on a regular basis.

But it didn't take long for his new life in the United States to lose its luster. During the 2000 season, Baddeley struggled to keep the pace and made the cut just once in nine starts. Perhaps the best moment during that stretch on the PGA Tour was receiving a special invitation to play in the Masters (the youngest player to ever receive such an honor) and the thrilling opportunity to play a round with Tiger Woods. Otherwise, a tie for fifty-seventh place at the Honda Classic was the one consolation in an otherwise disappointing season.

"This was going to be the best year of my life," Baddeley remembers. "This is where I wanted to be. This is where I'd dreamed of being for six years. I came over and in ten months I wanted to quit the game. It turned out to be the worst year of my life."

In 2001, Baddeley regained his winning stroke in time to capture the Greg Norman Holden International—a tournament hosted by and named after his boyhood hero and mentor. He also played in nine PGA Tour events that year, but barely fared better than the year before—by making two cuts. At that point, any reasonable golfer might have stressed out over form, training, or even equipment. Instead, Baddeley says it was an unusual life decision that sparked positive change.

"In 2002, I felt like God was calling me to take a dating vow," Baddeley says. "I felt like He was asking me to give up dating for a season. So for the next six months, I didn't go out with any girls. I did it without even thinking. That was the point where God really got a hold of me. That's where I really started to press in and seek Him."

Baddeley stayed in touch with his pastor from Australia, who mentored him through the process by email. Throughout the six months, he learned invaluable nuggets of wisdom about dating and about himself. But most importantly, Baddeley began experiencing a personal relationship with God like never before.

"From then on, I have been growing closer to the Lord," he says. "It was during that time of committing to Him and learning more about what the Bible said and about God that I learned how personable God is and how much He enjoys someone who is committed to Him. To maintain the vow and not break it, I had to be obedient, and it was through the obedience that I learned so much."

Not only did Baddeley grow spiritually and emotionally during those six months, but he also found that his golf game began improving as well. On the 2002 Nationwide Tour, he finished runner-up in three tournaments and earned his way onto the PGA Tour by placing tenth on the circuit's money list. Baddeley admits that the Nationwide Tour wasn't exactly where he wanted to be, but quickly realized that God had orchestrated the location and timing all along.

"That point was the best year of my life," Baddeley recalls. "Having a strong relationship with the Lord allowed me to have peace and happiness and enjoyment. The difference was obviously in my improved relationship with Christ. My friends noticed too, and I was able to share with them that the difference was Jesus."

As Baddeley's relationship with God grew, so did his success on the PGA Tour. As a rookie in 2003, he claimed three top-ten finishes, including the Sony Open in Hawaii, where he lost a two-hole playoff to Ernie Els. In 2004, Baddeley again narrowly missed his first tour victory with a second-place finish to Heath Slocum at the Chrysler Classic of Tucson, but he did maintain his PGA status by finishing in the top 125 on the money list.

In 2005, Baddeley continued his slow rise as one of the tour's next young contenders. But the dating vow he had taken three years earlier—and the lessons learned from it—finally paid off when he married the love of his life, Richelle, on Easter Sunday.

"I know that everything's in His time," Baddeley says. "You've got the promises of the Word that all things work for the good. When things don't go your way, you can be like, *All right, there's something going on here.* 'Lord, show me what You're trying to teach me.' The promises in the Word are what give you so much peace."

For Baddeley, 2006 was truly a break-out season. One year and one day after his wedding, he claimed his first PGA Tour title at the Verizon Heritage. The Sunday morning before the final round, Baddeley spoke at a sunrise service near the eighteenth green. After the win, his faith in Jesus became the centerpiece of every interview.

The 2007 season was even more successful, with a second PGA Tour victory at the FBR Open in Phoenix. Baddeley ended the year with more than $3 million in tournament earnings and finished sixth in the inaugural FedEx Cup standings.

Four years later, Baddeley had another big year. He won the 2011 Northern Trust Open and finished fourteenth in the FedEx Cup standings. Baddeley also earned over $3 million for the second time in his career.

Suffice it to say, Baddeley has been at both ends of the spectrum. He has missed the cut and lost his shot at the big time. On the flipside, he has won prestigious tournaments, earned big paychecks, and has shared the course with golf's greatest players. The precarious balance between success and failure has helped the young Aussie fully understand the biblical truth found in Romans 8:38–39.

"Nothing can separate us from His love," Baddeley says. "You could shoot 85–85, and you can go to the prayer closet, and He's going to be there. He's still going to want to talk to you. He's still going to want to hold you. In this day and age, performance is something that people struggle with, and I struggle with it as well. I wouldn't say I'm immune to it at all. There are times that you put a value on your performance."

In those times when Baddeley is tempted to let the insecurities of human nature creep back into his heart, he reminds himself of his personal definition of integrity: "To live according to God's Word."

Baddeley's first real-life examples of biblical integrity were his parents. More recently, he has relied on the models found in his wife, Richelle, and in close friend John Bevere—a noted author, speaker, and minister. Others that Baddeley has learned from include fellow PGA star Tom Lehman, longtime PGA chaplain Larry Moody, and Tommy Barnett, senior pastor at First Assembly of God in Phoenix. And one of the biggest lessons he's extrapolated from that impressive cast of characters is the importance of maintaining a high level of integrity in order to open the door to people's hearts.

"Live what you preach," Baddeley says. "As a Christian, you're always held under a microscope. You really have to be careful. You've got to live upright and holy. That's the biggest witnessing tool. It's just what James [2:26] is saying: 'Faith without works is dead.' You've got to live what your faith is."

Baddeley says that his biggest tool in reaching others is simply telling them the testimony of his life. "They can't argue with it because it's my testimony," he adds. But even more important to Baddeley is that he constantly does his best to go where God is leading him, and that means listening to that ever-present Guide.

"I definitely want to listen to what's going on inside, what the Holy Spirit is trying to say," Baddeley says. "Then I just tell them about Jesus. I often start out talking about church. I'll ask them where they go to church, and if they don't go, it opens the door."

Baddeley knows too well that effective outreach can be strengthened or weakened by the believer's integrity or lack thereof. That's why one of his favorite passages of Scripture is 1 Peter 1:15–16: "But, as the One who called you is holy, you also are to be in all your conduct; for it is written, Be holy, because I am holy."

"I love this because it's the Lord's call on all our lives," Baddeley says. "He is our example. He is our standard. He is who we need in our life to live a life of integrity and one that pleases God. I am supposed to strive to live my life like Jesus did."

One thing Baddeley has come to understand early in his life is the importance of commitment. It requires commitment to excellence in training and practice in order to become an elite golfer. It likewise requires commitment to make a marriage work. And commitment especially applies when it comes to one's character and the upholding of one's relationship with God.

"You need to be committed to walking in integrity and walking in God's commands," he says. "I feel what challenges me is that I need to be ready to be committed all the time, not some of the time, but 100 percent of the time. I need to be committed to integrity and God's commands, because that's what He expects from us. I feel like it's also important to make sure my heart is committed daily to walking along the right path."

According to Baddeley, the blessings that come from a life of integrity are innumerable and can be found in the here and now and in the ever after. But just as countless as those gifts can be, the dangers of turning from God's holiness are likewise immeasurable and something that all followers of Christ should avoid at all costs.

"By breaking commitments, we sin against God and against what He calls us to be," Baddeley says. "When we allow sin to enter our life by breaking commitments, we give the devil a foothold in our life. The more we sin, the easier it becomes, and the more of a habit it becomes. Then before we know it, we are walking in the wrong direction, and our integrity is no longer intact; and we are living a life that does not please God."

In the world of high-stakes professional sports, Baddeley has seen the highest highs and the lowest lows. He knows the difference between a life that relies on God and a life that trusts in oneself, and his level of commitment is no longer determined by external facts of life. That's why he says the best way to learn about integrity—and the most effective tools for a long-term spiritual commitment—is simply to read the pages of God's Word and to spend significant amounts of time in prayer.

"By doing this, God's Word becomes implanted in our heart," Baddeley says.

"When that happens, we are able to live a life of integrity and a life that pleases God. When we commit ourselves to being obedient to God's Word, we can all walk in a life of integrity."

Training Time

1. Read 2 Timothy 1:7. Can you describe some situations that cause you to worry? What reassurance does this Scripture give you for times like that? What is the significance of Jesus's reference to the spirits of "power, love, and sound judgment"?

2. Baddeley tells about a dating vow he took in 2002 that led to him not dating for six months. Has God ever taken you to extreme measures? If so, what kind of impact did they have on your relationship with Him?

3. Baddeley says, "By breaking commitments, we sin against God and against what He calls us to be."

What is the connection between commitment and integrity? What are some ways that you can stay accountable to your commitments?

4. Read Psalm 27:4. What does this passage suggest was the key behind David's devotion to God? How can you take David's example of commitment—in spite of his imperfection—and apply it to your life?

5. Read Philippians 3:13–14. Why do you think it is dangerous to dwell too much on the past? How does this passage inspire you to focus on the future? What part does commitment and integrity play in this process of pursuing "the prize promised by God's heavenly call in Christ Jesus"?

6

Character Counts

John Wooden
*Former UCLA Men's
Basketball Head Coach*

Blessed are the pure in heart, because they will see God.

Matthew 5:8

When wealth is lost, nothing is lost; when health is lost, something is lost; when character is lost, all is lost.

Billy Graham

One of Coach John Wooden's favorite Bible figures was Job. That might seem an odd choice for the man known for leading the UCLA Bruins to a record-smashing ten NCAA men's basketball championships, producing a slew of All-Americans and developing NBA stars such as Lew Alcindor (now Kareem Abdul Jabbar), Bill Walton, Walt Hazzard, Marques Johnson, and Henry Bibby.

But for the people who knew Wooden best, the choice isn't the least bit surprising, as can be extracted from one of the Bible's most straightforward passages: "There was a man in the country of Uz named Job. He was a man of perfect integrity, who feared God and turned away from evil" (Job 1:1).

That verse might seem simple on the surface, but the unique events of Job's life truly make his pursuit of integrity compelling. Because of Job's character, God had placed a hedge of protection around him and his family. He was blessed with health, wealth, and prosperity. But Satan questioned that faithfulness, so he asked for an opportunity to test Job and find out if he truly loved God.

Satan attacked Job with great sickness and immense poverty. He even took the lives of his children. While Job cried out to God and questioned his fate, this man of integrity never turned his back on the Lord, and ultimately he found a way to worship

God despite the traumatic circumstances. Eventually, Satan was vanquished from Job's life. Job's health was restored, and his material possessions were increased.

Like Job, who struggled in his faith during those hardships, Wooden (who died at the age of 99 in 2010) candidly admitted that there were times in his life when he failed to live up to the highest standards of integrity. While those moments were few and far between, he always learned from his mistakes and used them to not only better his own life but also the lives of those around him.

"At UCLA, I was tempted to be dishonest many times," Wooden once said. "Mostly I resisted, but there was one situation of which I am not very proud. An opposing coach repeatedly sent the wrong shooter to the free-throw line. Since the opposing coach got away with this illegal maneuver, I tried it too. But I was not so good at being stealthy—and I got caught. I regret giving in to temptation, not only because I got caught but primarily because I did not stay true to my standards."

Wooden also had a smoking habit that began during his World War II military service and plagued him early in his coaching career. He would quit during basketball season, and he never smoked in front of his players. But he felt convicted and realized that he needed to do a better job teaching the impressionable athletes not just about basketball but also about living a life of integrity.

"A leader's most powerful ally is his or her own example," Wooden said. "There is hypocrisy to the phrase, 'Do as I say, not as I do.' I refused to make demands on my boys that I wasn't willing to live out in my own life. Leadership from a base of hypocrisy undermines respect, and if people don't respect you, they won't willingly follow you."

Wooden's standards came straight from the Bible, which he began reading as a teenager. By the time he was in college, he was reading it on a daily basis. This habit continued on throughout his fifty-three-year marriage to his wife, Nellie (she passed away in 1985).

Wooden dove into the Bible because he enjoyed spending time in God's Word. To him, it was never the arduous task that sadly skews most Christians' perception about reading the Bible. Instead, Wooden's joyful participation in Bible study helped him to understand the purpose of God's commandments and empowered him to live out the truth found in Psalm 119:11: "I have treasured Your word in my heart so that I may not sin against You."

"The Lord created each of us to be unique, and, because of that, many of us have differing values," Wooden said. "But I believe God put some absolutes in place. The Ten Commandments reflect some of His absolutes. When we violate those absolutes, we fail as people of integrity."

According to Wooden, one of the most important pillars of integrity is honesty, which he famously described as "doing the things that we know are right and not giving into the temptation to do the things that we know are wrong."

Of course, Wooden fully realized that honesty isn't a natural occurrence in the human DNA. Once Adam and Eve sinned in the Garden of Eden by disobeying God and then lying about it, mankind was instantly plagued with the hereditary disease of dishonesty. Jesus pointed out this harsh reality to the religious leaders of the day when He rebuked their self-righteous attitudes in Matthew 12:34, saying, "How can you speak good things when you are evil? For the mouth speaks from the overflow of the heart."

It's the condition of the heart that produces truth or lies, good or bad choices, or healthy or destructive behaviors. But the root cause can always be traced back to what a person has allowed into his or her heart through the portals of the ears and the eyes, which are then filtered through the mind. "Integrity in its simplest form is purity of intention," Wooden said. "It's keeping a clean conscience. Purity of intention is really a reflection of the heart. The heart of a person with integrity always wants to do what's right, once he or she is sure what 'right' is."

In his forty years of coaching high school and college basketball, Wooden saw every kind of personality and character type imaginable. He coached players who had something he calls "selective integrity," but he also worked with athletes who had a firm grasp on the concept. At the end of the day, it was the ones who chose the narrow road who received the greatest rewards.

"When we have integrity, we are not going to do anything that will be demeaning to anybody else, either on or off the court," Wooden said. "And with integrity, we will never consider letting our teammates down. I think I can safely say that the more the quality of integrity was represented in the best seven or eight players on each of my teams, the better their team play became."

While Wooden enjoyed great success based on the team play produced by young men with outstanding integrity, winning championships and personal accolades never measured up to the spiritual blessings that accompanied the life of Christ-centered character. In fact, it was Jesus Himself who in the famed Sermon on the Mount said, "The pure in heart are blessed, for they will see God" (Matt. 5:8).

But beyond the eternal ramifications of honesty and integrity, Wooden firmly believed that there are immense benefits here on Earth for those who choose to embrace truth at all times. "Honesty is not only the best policy, but it is also the best therapy," Wooden said. "Telling the truth and being true to ourselves not only enhance our relations with others and with God, but they also make us feel good about ourselves."

Training Time

1. Read Job 1:1. When you're dealing with tough times, what effect do those circumstances tend to have on your character? What gives you strength and peace of mind during such trials?

2. Read Psalm 119:11. What truth found in this passage is the key to living with integrity? What are some specific ways that your study of the Bible has helped you make good decisions in life?

3. Wooden said, "Integrity in its simplest form is purity of intention." Do you agree with that statement? Read Matthew 12:34. What commentary do you think Jesus was trying to make about the condition of the heart with regard to one's actions? Do you think it is possible to serve others, but with wrong motivations?

4. What are some tough decisions that could challenge one's integrity? How does one's willingness (or lack of willingness) to face the consequences of such a decision speak to the issue of motive and intent (or purity of heart)?

5. Read Matthew 5:8. What does this Scripture state is the ultimate benefit of having a pure heart? How might that blessing come to fruition in this life? What about in the next life?

Thanks

Fellowship of Christian Athletes would like to give honor and glory to our Lord and Savior Jesus Christ for the opportunities we have been given to impact so many lives and for everyone who has come alongside us in this ministry.

The four core values are at the heart of what we do and teach. Many people have helped make this series of books on these values a reality. We extend a huge thanks to Chad Bonham for his many hours of hard work in interviewing, writing, compiling, and editing. These books would not have been possible without him. Thanks also to Chad's wife, Amy, and his three sons, Lance, Cole, and Quinn.

We also want to thank the following people and groups for their vital contributions: Les Steckel, Tony Dungy, Jackie Cook, the Wooden family, Aaron Baddeley, Tamika Catchings, Rocco Grimaldi, Rick Randazzo, and FCA Hockey.

Thanks to the entire FCA staff, who every day faithfully serve coaches and athletes. Thanks to our CEO and president, Les Steckel, for believing in this project. Thanks to the National Support Center staff: Jeff Martin, Shea Vailes, and Dan Britton. Thanks also to everyone at Revell Books.

Impacting the World for Christ Through Sports

Since 1954, the Fellowship of Christian Athletes has challenged athletes and coaches to impact the world for Jesus Christ. FCA is cultivating Christian principles in local communities nationwide by encouraging, equipping, and empowering others to serve as examples and make a difference. FCA reaches more than two million people annually on the professional, college, high school, junior high, and youth levels. Through FCA's Four Cs of Ministry—Coaches, Campus, Camp, and Community—and the shared passion for athletics and faith, lives are changed for current and future generations.

Fellowship of Christian Athletes
8701 Leeds Road • Kansas City, MO 64129
www. fca.org • fca@fca.org • 1-800-289-0909

Fellowship
of Christian Athletes
Competitor's Creed

I am a Christian first and last.

I am created in the likeness of God Almighty to bring Him glory.

I am a member of Team Jesus Christ.

I wear the colors of the cross.

I am a Competitor now and forever.

I am made to strive, to strain, to stretch and to succeed in the arena of competition.

I am a Christian Competitor and as such, I face my challenger with the face of Christ.

I do not trust in myself.

I do not boast in my abilities or believe in my own strength.

I rely solely on the power of God.

I compete for the pleasure of my Heavenly Father, the honor of Christ and the reputation of the Holy Spirit.

My attitude on and off the field is above reproach—my conduct beyond criticism.

Whether I am preparing, practicing or playing, I submit to God's authority and those He has put over me.

I respect my coaches, officials, teammates, and competitors out of respect for the Lord.

My body is the temple of Jesus Christ.

I protect it from within and without.

Nothing enters my body that does not honor the Living God.

My sweat is an offering to my Master. My soreness is a sacrifice to my Savior.

I give my all—all the time.

I do not give up. I do not give in. I do not give out.

I am the Lord's warrior—a competitor by conviction and a disciple of determination.

I am confident beyond reason because my confidence lies in Christ.

The results of my effort must result in His glory.

Let the competition begin.

Let the glory be God's.

© Fellowship of Christian Athletes, 2015

Sign the Creed • Go to www.fca.org

Fellowship
of Christian Athletes
Coach's Mandate

Pray as though nothing of eternal value is going to happen in my athletes' lives unless God does it.

Prepare each practice and game as giving "my utmost for His highest."

Seek not to be served by my athletes for personal gain, but seek to serve them as Christ served the church.

Be satisfied not with producing a good record, but with producing good athletes.

Attend carefully to my private and public walk with God, knowing that the athlete will never rise to a standard higher than that being lived by the coach.

Exalt Christ in my coaching, trusting the Lord will then draw athletes to Himself.

Desire to have a growing hunger for God's Word, for personal obedience, for fruit of the spirit and for saltiness in competition.

Depend solely upon God for transformation—one athlete at a time.

Preach Christ's word in a Christ-like demeanor, on and off the field of competition.

Recognize that it is impossible to bring glory to both myself and Christ at the same time.

Allow my coaching to exude the fruit of the Spirit, thus producing Christ-like athletes.

Trust God to produce in my athletes His chosen purposes, regardless of whether the wins are readily visible.

Coach with humble gratitude, as one privileged to be God's coach.

Impacting The World
For Christ Through Sports

Since 1954, the Fellowship of Christian Athletes has challenged athletes and coaches to impact the world for Jesus Christ. FCA is cultivating Christian principles in local communities nationwide by encouraging, equipping, and empowering others to serve as examples and make a difference. FCA reaches more than 2 million people annually on the professional, college, high school, junior high, and youth levels. Through FCA's Four Cs of Ministry—coaches, campus, camps, and community—and the shared passion for athletics and faith, lives are changed for current and future generations.

Fellowship of Christian Athletes
8701 Leeds Road • Kansas City, MO 64129
www.fca.org • fca@fca.org • 1-800-289-0909